THE HEALTHY
SALAD
COOKBOOK

Tamara Johnston

Sweetwater Press
Florence, Alabama

Published by Sweetwater Press
P.O. Box 1855
Florence, Alabama 35631

Produced by The Triangle Group, Ltd.
227 Park Avenue
Hoboken, NJ 07030

Design: Tony Meisel
Special thanks to Risa Gary of Mikasa, New York
Origination and printing: Cronion S.A., Barcelona

Printed in Spain

ISBN 1-884822-01-0

Contents

Introduction

The greening of America has started . . . in the salad bowl! Never before have so many people been appreciative of salads, and not the old standby of iceberg lettuce with gloppy dressings either. Salads have become not only mainstays to a meal, but often centerpieces as well.

A salad can encompass almost any ingredient: meat, fish or cheese, vegetables, fruits, grains, even bread. It can be mixed with dressings sweet, sour, salty or tart.

Most importantly, salads not only taste good, they are also good for you. Generally speaking, they are low in fat and cholesterol, light yet satisfying, high in necessary roughage and quick and easy to prepare.

The salads in this book are, without exception, designed to fulfill these goals. Replacing a full lunch or dinner with one of these salads can go a long way to keeping you trimmer and thinner. Dressed with moderation and accompanied by a hunk of good, crusty bread (no butter, please), these salads will fulfill the necessary nutritional requirements while exciting your taste buds.

No attempt has been made to follow the various dietary strictures to the letter. Rather, common sense and a sense of proportion are what we should strive for. Balance in your menu planning and the development of intelligent eating habits will make your diet a life-long pleasure, rather than a never-ending series of fearful expectations.

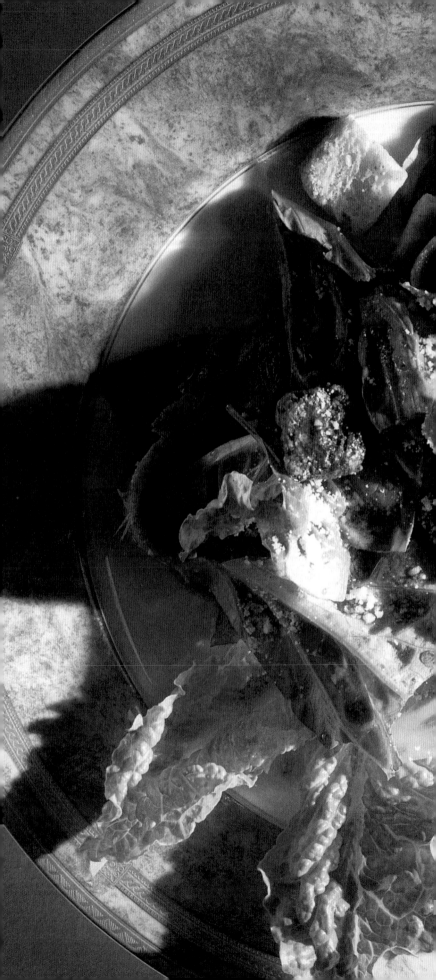

Caesar Salad

Not a salad in the tradition of Julius, Rome 48 BC, but in the tradition of Caesar Cardini, Tiajuana, circa 1920. Cardini was a restaurateur whose clients were the early legends of Hollywood. This salad is best when done in the theatrical tradition in which it was invented. You make it in front of your guests.

2 large heads of romaine lettuce
1 garlic clove, minced
1/2 cup olive oil, preferably extra virgin olive oil
1/2 teaspoon freshly ground black pepper
1/2 teaspoon salt
2 tablespoons fresh lemon juice
1/2 cup freshly grated Parmesan cheese
6 to 8 anchovy fillets
1/4 teaspoon Worcestershire sauce
2 eggs, raw or hard-cooked, chopped
1 1/2 cups garlic croutons

Pull the lettuce leaves from the stalks and tear them into bite-size pieces. Put the garlic and oil in jar with a tight fitting lid. Cover and shake well. Set the jar aside. Put the lettuce in a large salad bowl and the rest of the ingredients into individual bowls.

In front of your guests, grind the pepper over the lettuce leaves with a pepper mill. Pour the oil on the lettuce leaves and gently toss, enough to coat each leaf. Sprinkle the lettuce with salt. Add the lemon, Parmesan cheese, anchovy fillets and Worcestershire sauce. Gently toss the salad twice. If you are using raw eggs break them into the salad. If the eggs are hard-cooked add them in a dramatic fashion. Toss with croutons and serve.
Serves 6-8.

Orange & Greens Salad

Refreshing in sight and taste, this salad is an excellent accompaniment to roast lamb or pork. This salad goes well with dry white wine.

1/4 head red leaf lettuce
1/4 head Boston lettuce
2 navel oranges
1 cup carrots cut into strips
1/4 sultanas or currants
3/4 cup Paprika Dressing

Tear lettuce into bite-size pieces. Arrange them in a salad bowl. Peel the oranges and divide them into segments. Cut each segment into halves or thirds. Add the orange pieces, carrots and sultanas to the salad bowl. Toss. Add the Paprika Dressing and toss again. Serves 4.

Garden Mixed Green Salad

Almost any fresh salad green may be substituted for those called for in this recipe. It is a substantial salad that can be served alone as light summertime lunch or with veal and beef roast dinners.

1 head Boston or garden lettuce
1 head romaine lettuce
3 Belgian endives
1/4 cup celery, chopped
3 hard-cooked eggs, sliced
1/2 cup watercress, chopped and stems removed
1/2 medium onion, sliced into rings
2 large tomatoes, peeled and cut into wedges
1/2 cup pickled beets, cut into strips
2 tablespoons fresh parsley, chopped
1 1/3 cups Modern Vinaigrette

Line a salad bowl with some lettuce leaves. Tear the remaining lettuce leaves into bite-size pieces. Add them to the salad bowl. Cut the endives into bite-size pieces and add to the salad bowl. Add the celery, eggs watercress, onion rings and tomatoes to the salad bowl. Toss gently, pour the Modern Vinaigrette on the salad and toss again. Add the beets and parsley just before serving. Serves 6-8.

Mixed Greens & Mushrooms

The Italian Dressing and roasted pine nuts make this salad extra special.

1/2 cup pine nuts (pignoli)
2 heads of Boston lettuce
2 Belgian endives
1 small head radicchio
1/2 cup steamed small mushrooms, sliced
1/3 cup Italian Dressing

Preheat the oven to 350° F. Put the pine nuts on a baking sheet and toast them in the oven for 8-10 minutes or until brown. Tear the lettuce and radicchio into bite-size pieces. Cut the endive into thin slices. Put the greens into a large salad bowl. Add the pine nuts and mushrooms. Pour the dressing over the greens and toss well. Serves 4.

Fennel Salad with Pernod Vinaigrette

The anise-tasting leaves of the fennel plant lend an interesting tang to a salad, especially when teamed with a Pernod Vinaigrette.

1 medium fennel
4 radishes, thinly sliced
2 oranges, peeled and sectioned
4 black olives, pitted and halved
3 tablespoons onion, minced
several torn feathers from the fennel stalk
1/2 cup Vinaigrette
6 tablespoons olive oil
3 tablespoons cider vinegar
1 teaspoon Pernod or anisette
1/4 teaspoon salt
1/8 teaspoon cayenne pepper

Slice the bulb and stalks of the fennel into rings. Place in a serving bowl. Arrange the radishes, orange sections, olives, onion, and torn fennel feathers around the sliced fennel rings. In a mixing bowl, whisk together the oil, vinegar, Pernod, salt and cayenne pepper. Pour over the salad and serve. Serves 4.

Snow Pea Salad

The bright green snow pea pods in this salad make a colorful accompaniment to fish and chicken dishes. Bamboo shoots, water chestnuts, Chinese cabbage, and snow peas are all staple Asian foods and should be available at better supermarkets.

24 snow peas, fresh or frozen
6-8 marinated artichoke hearts, drained and chopped
1/2 cup bamboo shoots, drained
12 water chestnuts, sliced
3/4 cup Chinese cabbage, shredded
8 large mushrooms, thinly sliced
1 cup Chinese Dressing
4-6 parsley sprigs

In a pan of lightly salted boiling water, cook the snow peas for one minute or until they turn bright green. Drain well. Rinse the snow peas in very cold water and drain again. Put the snow peas, artichoke hearts, bamboo shoots, water chestnuts, Chinese cabbage and mushrooms in a bowl. Toss. Add the Chinese Dressing and toss again. Garnish with parsley and serve. Serves 6.

Cobb Salad

This is a version of the popular salad served at the Brown Derby restaurant in Hollywood during the 1930s and 1940s. It was invented by the noted American humorist, writer and actor Irving Cobb. There are many variations on the original recipe, but they all have one thing in common: the ingredients are all cut into tiny pieces.

1/2 head iceberg lettuce, torn in pieces
1 head Belgian endive
1/3 head romaine lettuce, torn into bite-size pieces
2/3 bunch chicory, torn in pieces
2/3 bunch watercress, torn into sprigs
2 medium-size tomatoes, peeled and diced
3 cups poached chicken breasts, diced
1 green pepper, seeded and finely chopped
1 sweet red pepper, seeded and finely chopped
1/4 cup crisply cooked bacon, crumbled
1/4 cup scallions, minced
1 1/3 cups Modern Vinaigrette

On a large serving platter, arrange the iceberg lettuce, chicory, endive, romaine lettuce and watercress. Add the remaining ingredients, except for the dressing, in either lines, layers or piles. The choice is yours. Chill for 30 minutes. Add the dressing just before serving. Do not toss. Serves 6-8.

Asian Salad with Peanut Dressing

Peanut dressings are very popular in Indonesia. This salad is a distant variation of the Indonesian favorite *Gado Gado*. Although it requires some cooking it is served at room temperature, usually during the hot months of summer.

2 cups romaine lettuce, shredded
1 cup spinach, shredded
4 cups bean sprouts
2 cups green beans, cut into 1-inch pieces
1 cup carrots, sliced into strips
1 cup cucumber, sliced
5 tablespoons peanut oil, vegetable oil may be substituted

Peanut Dressing
1/2 cup onion, minced
1 cup water
3 tablespoons red wine vinegar
1 1/2 teaspoons sugar
3 tablespoons peanuts, ground
1/2 cup peanut butter
1 teaspoon chili powder
1/4 teaspoon salt

Drop the vegetables and lettuce in boiling water. As soon as the water returns to a boil, but no more than ninety seconds later, remove the vegetables and immediately run under very cold water. Drain and place in a salad bowl. In a small skillet sauté the onion in oil until soft. Add the water, vinegar, sugar and ground peanuts. Stir for a few seconds. Stir in the peanut butter, chili powder and salt. Continue stirring until the dressing is well combined. This may take between 4 and 5 minutes. Lower the heat and simmer for another minute. Remove and let cool. Pour the dressing on the salad and serve. Serves 4-6.

California Salad

This salad is very popular in the Golden State where tomatoes and oranges grow all year round. It is a good accompaniment to meat entrees.

1 pound spinach, leaves torn into bite-size pieces
    and stems removed
1/2 head chicory, torn into bite-size pieces
1 head Boston lettuce, torn into bite-size pieces
1/2 head romaine lettuce, torn into bite-size pieces
2 tomatoes, seeded and diced
1 1/2 cups mandarin orange slices
2 large mushrooms, sliced
2 tablespoons capers, drained
2 tablespoons honey
1 cup Paprika Dressing

Put all the lettuces in a salad bowl and chill for one hour. Just before serving, remove the salad from the refrigerator and add the tomatoes, oranges, mushrooms and capers. Toss lightly. In a jar with tight fitting lid add the Paprika Dressing and honey. Shake until the honey has combined with the dressing. Pour the dressing on the salad. Serves 8.

Cachcombar

Serve this Indian tomato and onion salad for a refreshing end to a rich meal. The salad contains onions, lots of them. Garnish each plate with a few sprigs of fresh parsley. Parsley is a very effective natural breath freshener.

1 teaspoon fresh ginger, minced
1 tablespoon fresh coriander or parsley, chopped
1/4 cup lime juice
1/4 teaspoon salt
1/4 teaspoon freshly ground black pepper
3 large tomatoes, seeded and sliced
2 medium-size white onions, sliced into rings
1/4 cup green peppers, chopped
2 hot green chili peppers, seeded and coarsely chopped

Put the ginger, coriander, lime juice, salt and pepper in a jar with a tightly fitting lid. Cover and shake until the salt dissolves. Arrange the tomatoes and onions in rows on a serving dish. Sprinkle with both types of peppers. Pour the lime juice dressing over the salad and let stand for 30 minutes before serving. Serves 4.

Moroccan Pepper Salad

A favorite among Moroccans, this salad goes well with
meat stews and couscous.

6 large sweet green peppers
6 large tomatoes
2 medium-size onions
1/3 cup olive oil
3 tablespoons fresh lemon juice
1 tablespoon ground cumin
1/4 teaspoon hot red pepper flakes, crushed
3/4 teaspoon fresh coriander, chopped
6 black olives
6 anchovy fillets

Preheat the broiler. Put the peppers and tomatoes on a
baking sheet and cook, turning the peppers and tomatoes
occasionally, until the skins begin to blister. Remove the
vegetables from the broiler and set aside to cool. Remove
the skins and seeds from the peppers and tomatoes. Chop
the tomatoes, peppers and onions. Combine them in a
salad bowl. In a large jar with tight fitting lid put the olive
oil, lemon juice, cumin, red pepper flakes and coriander.
Shake well. Pour the dressing over the salad and toss.
Marinate in the refrigerator for 1 1/2 hours, tossing
occasionally. Remove the salad from the refrigerator and
garnish with olives and anchovies. Serves 6-8.

German Potato Salad

An American potato salad that still bears the name of its country of origin. Serve it with chicken, beef or ham.

4 scallions, minced
1 garlic clove, minced
1 teaspoon capers, drained
2 tablespoons fresh dill, chopped
2 tablespoons fresh parsley, chopped
1 teaspoon salt
1 teaspoon freshly ground black pepper
5 tablespoons vegetable oil
3 tablespoons white wine vinegar
1 tablespoon beef stock
1/2 teaspoon sugar

Cook the potatoes with their skins in a large pot of lightly salted boiling water. Drain well and either peel and dice the potatoes, or leave the small potatoes whole and unpeeled. Put the potatoes in a salad bowl and add the green onions, garlic, capers, dill, and parsley. Toss lightly. In a large jar with tight fitting lid put the salt, pepper, oil, vinegar, beef stock and sugar. Shake until the sugar and salt dissolve. Pour the dressing over the salad and toss. Let stand at room temperature for 1 1/2 hours before serving. Serves 6.

Ham & Vegetable Pasta Salad

A good way to use leftover ham and an excellent summer-time main course. Serve this salad with a German Mosel or Rhine white wine.

1 pound pasta shapes, cooked
2 tablespoons extra virgin olive oil
1 cup uncooked peas
1 cup raw carrots, sliced
1 cup broccoli florets
1 cup cooked ham, cubed
1/4 cup grated Parmesan cheese
2 tablespoons fresh parsley, chopped
1 cup Italian Dressing
1 teaspoon freshly ground black pepper

Put the cooked pasta in a salad bowl and add the olive oil. Toss to coat the pasta well. Cook the peas, carrots and broccoli in a large pan of boiling water until just tender, about 8-10 minutes. Drain and rinse with cold water. Drain again. Add the vegetables, ham, cheese and parsley to the pasta. Toss until well mixed. Add the Italian Dressing and lightly toss. Serves 6.

Crab Meat Salad,
Hot Caper Dressing

The caper dressing in this salad will work equally well over cooked lobster meat. Serve the salad with a dry white wine for brunch or as a first course at dinner.

5 cups romaine lettuce, torn into bite-size pieces
1 1/2 cups cooked crab meat, still warm
1/2 cup olive oil
3 tablespoons red wine vinegar
3 tablespoons drained capers
1 garlic clove, finely chopped
1/4 teaspoon salt
1/2 teaspoon dried oregano
freshly ground black pepper to taste

Put the romaine lettuce and the crab meat in a salad bowl. Loosely mix and set aside. In a saucepan combine the olive oil, vinegar, capers, garlic, salt, oregano, and pepper. Heat just to the boiling point and quickly remove the saucepan from the flame. Pour the warm dressing over the lettuce and crab meat. Toss well and serve at once. Serves 4.

Spanish Chicken Salad

Leftover chicken returns to table as an entrée salad. It is a complete meal made from a very flexible recipe. Feel free to add other crisply cooked or raw vegetables to it.

3 cups cooked chicken, shredded
1/2 cup salami, cubed
3 medium-size boiled potatoes, peeled and diced
1 green pepper, seeded and coarsely chopped
1/2 cup pimentos, chopped
1 cup cooked green peas
2 radishes, thinly sliced
2 tablespoons capers, drained
1/2 cup pimento-stuffed green olives, quartered
3 tablespoons dry sherry
1/2 cup olive oil, preferably extra virgin olive oil
1/4 cup white wine vinegar
1/4 teaspoon ground white pepper
1 large head Boston lettuce
2 hard-cooked eggs, chopped
6-8 cooked asparagus spears
8 fresh parsley sprigs
1 medium-size onion, sliced into rings

Put the chicken, salami, potato, chopped pepper, pimentos, green peas, radishes, capers and olives in a mixing bowl. Toss once. Put the sherry, olive oil, vinegar and white pepper in a jar with a tightly fitting lid. Cover and shake until well mixed. Pour the dressing over the salad and toss again. Cover and chill for four hours. Line a serving platter with lettuce leaves. Add the chopped eggs to the salad in the mixing bowl and toss lightly. Drain any excess dressing from the bottom of the mixing bowl and transfer the salad to the serving plate. Garnish with the asparagus spears, parsley sprigs and onion rings.
Serves 6-8.

Curried Apricot
& Chicken Salad

A chilled white wine is a good accompaniment to this main-course salad. If your tastes run to spicier foods, add 1 tablespoon of ground cardamom and 1/8 teaspoon of cayenne pepper in with the curry powder.

4 chicken breasts, skinned and boned
4 tablespoons sweet butter
1 cup unflavored yogurt
1/4 cup curry powder
1 teaspoon salt
1/4 teaspoon freshly ground black pepper
1/2 pound seedless green grapes
2 cups dried apricots, cut in strips
2 cups mandarin orange segments
1 cup cashews
2 tablespoons apricot liqueur
6-8 lettuce leaves

Cut the chicken breasts into 1-inch cubes. Melt the butter in a large skillet. Add the chicken and cook over a moderate to low heat, turning often, until the cubes are firm, but not brown. This may take 7-10 minutes. Transfer the chicken to a large mixing bowl using a slotted spoon. Combine the yogurt and curry powder in a separate small bowl. Add the yogurt and curry to the chicken in the mixing bowl. Season with salt and pepper, and more curry, if desired. Add the remaining ingredients, except the lettuce, to the chicken. Toss until all the components are well coated. Cover and refrigerate for at least one hour. Line a serving dish with the lettuce leaves and serve. Serves 4-6.

Mussel Salad

Mussels are one of the best sources of low-fat protein around. They are also very cheap. This makes a main course salad perfect for a summer's eve.

6 pounds mussels
1 cup white wine
2 cloves garlic, peeled
1 large onion, finely chopped
1 red pepper, peeled, seeded and cut in strips
1 cup olive oil
1/4 cup wine vinegar
1/2 teaspoon freshly ground black pepper
1 tablespoon capers, drained and rinsed

Scrub the mussels well, removing the beards. Place them in a large pot with the white wine, garlic, onion and red pepper. Bring to a boil, pot covered, and cook until the mussels open, a matter of only a few minutes. When cool enough to handle, remove the mussels from their shells, discarding any that haven't opened or have broken shells, and place in a large bowl. Strain the broth and add the remaining vegetables to the mussels. Add the oil, vinegar, pepper and capers and toss well. Let cool to room temperature before serving. If you must refrigerate this salad, let it stand for an hour out of the refrigerator before serving for the flavors to develop. Serves 4.

Sprout & Walnut Salad

The crunchiness of sprouts—bean, alfalfa or pea—
coupled with the richness of walnut meats makes an
unusual and luxurious salad.

6 cups sprouts
3/4 cup walnut meats, roughly chopped
1 cup Modern Vinaigrette

Place sprouts and walnuts in a salad bowl. Add dressing
and toss lightly. Serves 4.

Tricolor Pepper Salad

Peppers—green, red and yellow—are often overlooked as salad ingredients. Providing they are cooked and peeled, they will upset no stomachs. To peel them with ease, place the peppers directly over a stove burner and char, turning often. Run charred peppers under cold water, then peel.

3 green peppers, peeled, seeded and roughly chopped
3 red peppers, peeled, seeded and roughly chopped
3 yellow peppers, peeled, seeded and roughly chopped
1 large onion, chopped finely
3/4 cup olive oil
2 tablespoons lemon juice
1 small can flat anchovy filets
1/2 cup black olives

In a serving bowl, combine the peppers with the olive oil and lemon juice. Toss well. Drain the anchovies and arrange over the top of the salad. Scatter the black olives over all. Serves 4-6.

Chinese Pork Salad

2 cups mung bean or alfalfa sprouts
1 medium carrot, peeled and shredded
2 cups roast pork, shredded
2 tablespoons smooth peanut butter
3 tablespoons warm water
1/2 teaspoon salt
1 tablespoon sugar
1 teaspoon honey
1 tablespoon sesame oil
1 1/2 tablespoons white wine vinegar
1 tablespoon peanut oil
1 teaspoon Tabasco sauce
2 garlic cloves, minced
3 tablespoons scallions, chopped

Blanch the bean sprouts in separate pans of boiling water for about 10 seconds. Drain and immediately rinse in cold water. Drain and pat dry with paper towels. Line a serving plate with the sprouts and carrots. Make a mound of roast pork on top of the sprouts and carrots. In a jar with a tight fitting lid add the peanut butter and water. Cover and shake until the peanut butter has been completely diluted by the water. Add the remaining ingredients and shake again until well blended. Pour the dressing over the pork. Serves 4-6.

Clam & Pasta Salad

Although it looks like a plate of hot pasta with white clam sauce, this salad is really an easy to make, cool refreshing summer variation. Shrimp and/or mussels may be substituted or added according taste.

1/2 pound pasta shapes, cooked and drained
1/2 cup extra virgin olive oil
1/2 pound cooked clams, chopped
3 tablespoons fresh lemon juice
1 1/2 garlic cloves, minced
3 tablespoons fresh parsley, chopped
2 tablespoons fresh basil, chopped
1 tablespoon fresh mint, chopped
3 tablespoons freshly grated Parmesan cheese
1/2 teaspoon salt
1 teaspoon freshly ground black pepper

Put the pasta in a large salad bowl and add one tablespoon of the olive oil. Lightly toss, add the clams and toss again. Put the remaining olive oil, lemon juice and garlic in a jar with a tightly fitting lid. Cover and shake until well mixed. Add the parsley, basil, mint, Parmesan cheese, salt and pepper. Shake again until blended. Pour the dressing over the salad and toss again. Serve at once or chill up to two hours before serving. Serves 4-6.

Linguini Salad

This makes a perfect impromptu luncheon salad for summertime guests.

4 large tomatoes, seeded and coarsely chopped
1/4 cup marinated artichoke hearts, drained and chopped
4 teaspoons parsley, chopped
1 cup Italian Dressing
1 teaspoon Tabasco sauce
1 pound linguini

Put the tomatoes, artichoke hearts and parsley in a salad bowl. Add the Tabasco sauce to the Italian Dressing and pour over the tomatoes and artichoke hearts. Let stand at room temperature for one hour. Cook the linguini in a large pot of boiling water until just tender. Drain well and add the linguini to the salad bowl. Toss well and serve. Serves 4-6.

Italian Fontina Salad

Fontina is a mild, velvet-textured cheese produced in northern Italy. It combines well with other ingredients in a solid or melted state. Serve this salad with a light, dry red wine.

2 large yellow peppers, seeded and halved
2 large red peppers, seeded and halved
1/2 pound fontina cheese, diced
1/4 cup pitted green olives, thinly sliced
1/3 cup olive oil, preferably extra virgin
1 1/2 teaspoons Dijon-style mustard
3 tablespoons cream
1 tablespoon scallion, chopped
3/4 teaspoon salt
1 teaspoon freshly ground black pepper
1 tablespoon fresh parsley, chopped

Preheat the broiler. Place the peppers on a baking sheet and broil for 10 to 15 minutes or until the skins are blistered and slightly blackened. Remove the peppers from the heat. When the peppers are cool enough to handle, remove the blistered skin. Cut the peppers into thin strips and place in a serving bowl. Add the fontina cheese and olives. Toss once. In a large jar with tight fitting lid put the olive oil, mustard, cream, scallion, salt and black pepper. Shake until salt dissolves. Pour the dressing over the salad and toss. Chill the salad for one hour. Garnish with chopped parsley and serve. Serves 6.

Lentil & Feta Salad

Feta is a common cheese in the Middle East and Greece. It is readily available from cheese shops and better markets.

1 1/2 cups brown lentils
1 bay leaf
1/2 teaspoon dried basil
2 garlic cloves, crushed
1/2 cup celery, diced
1 small onion, chopped
1/2 cup fresh chives, chopped
3/4 cup feta cheese, crumbled
6 tablespoons extra virgin olive oil
3 tablespoons red wine vinegar
1/8 teaspoon oregano
1/2 teaspoon salt
1/2 teaspoon freshly ground black pepper

Put the lentils in a bowl and add two and half cups of water. Soak the lentils for two hours. Drain. In saucepan, put the soaked lentils and enough cold water to cover. Add the bay leaf, basil, and one garlic clove. Bring to a boil and simmer, covered, for 20 minutes. Add the celery and onion. Again, pour just enough water on the lentil mixture to cover. Cover the saucepan and cook for 10 more minutes. Drain and discard the bay leaf and garlic clove. Serves 6.

Chickpea Salad

Chickpeas add a nutty, satisfying quality to many dishes. Here, they are used in salad Provence-style with North African overtones.

1/4 cup raisins
2 1/2 cups cooked chickpeas
1/2 cup sweet red pepper, diced
1/2 cup green onions, finely chopped
2 tablespoons pimentos, chopped
3 tablespoons parsley, chopped
1/3 cup olive oil
3 tablespoons lemon juice
1/2 teaspoon dried thyme
1/2 teaspoon freshly ground black pepper

Soak the raisins in a small bowl in cold water to cover for 30 minutes; drain well. Combine the chickpeas, red pepper, raisins, green onion, pimentos and parsley in a salad bowl and toss. Put the olive oil, lemon juice, thyme and pepper in a jar with a tight-fitting lid. Cover and shake well until blended. Pour over the salad and toss well to coat. Chill for 1 hour. Serves 6.

Waldorf Salad

This enduring classic was first served at the famed Waldorf Astoria Hotel in New York as an appetizer. It's also good as an accompaniment to ham and pork.

3 tart apples, cored and diced (do not peel)
2 cups celery, chopped
1/2 cup walnuts, coarsely chopped
3 tablespoons raisins
3 tablespoons lemon juice
3/4 cup yogurt
1 teaspoon salt
1/2 teaspoon freshly ground black pepper

Place all in the ingredients in a mixing bowl and toss until well coated. Chill for 1 hour. Serve atop lettuce leaves on individual plates. Serves 4-6.

Classic French Vinaigrette

2 tablespoons wine vinegar
6 tablespoons olive oil, preferably extra virgin
1 teaspoon salt
1/8 teaspoon freshly ground pepper

Put the vinegar, salt and pepper in a small wooden salad bowl. Beat the mixture with a wire whisk or fork until the salt dissolves. Add the olive oil and beat until the mixture has a creamy texture. Let stand for 5 minutes, beat once more and pour over a mixed green salad. Makes 1/2 cup.

Modern Vinaigrette

3/4 cup olive oil, preferably extra virgin
2 tablespoons wine vinegar
1 tablespoon lemon juice
1 teaspoon mustard
1/4 teaspoon salt, or to taste
1/8 teaspoon freshly ground black pepper

Put the vinegar, lemon juice, mustard, salt and pepper in a jar with a tightly fitting lid. Cover the jar tightly and shake until the salt dissolves. Add the olive oil and shake again until well mixed. Let stand for 10 minutes and shake the jar one last time. Pour over a mixed green salad. Makes 1 cup.

Touch of Asia Dressing

2 tablespoons soy sauce
2 teaspoons water
1 whole green onion, minced
1/2 teaspoon sesame oil
1/4 teaspoon hot pepper chili oil
1 finely chopped garlic clove
1/4 teaspoon ground black pepper
3/4 cup peanut oil
7 teaspoons rice wine vinegar

Put the soy sauce, water, green onion, sesame oil, hot pepper oil, garlic and black pepper in a jar with a tightly fitting lid. Cover and shake until all the ingredients are blended. Add the peanut oil to the jar, cover and shake again. Let the mixture stand for two minutes. Add the vinegar to the jar. Cover tightly and shake well once more. Pour over salad. Makes 1 1/2 cups.

Chinese Dressing

1 tablespoon soy sauce
1 tablespoon oyster sauce
1 garlic clove coarsely chopped
1 teaspoon fresh ginger, chopped, or 2 teaspoons
    dried ginger powder
6 tablespoons rice wine vinegar
3/4 cup peanut oil (any light oil may be substituted)

Put the soy sauce, oyster sauce, garlic, ginger and vinegar into a food processor. Pulse the food processor for 3 seconds or until all the ingredients are well blended. Add the peanut oil and pulse again until the mixture has become smooth. Pour over salad. Makes 1 1/4 cups.

Paprika Dressing

1 tablespoon honey
1/2 teaspoon salt
1 1/2 tablespoons water
2 teaspoons paprika
1 tablespoon Dijon mustard
2/3 cup pure olive oil
4 tablespoons red wine vinegar
1/4 teaspoon freshly ground pepper

In a jar with tight fitting lid put the honey, salt and water. Shake until the salt and honey dissolve. Pour the honey water mixture into a food processor. Add the paprika, mustard and process for three seconds or until the ingredients are well blended. Add the olive oil, vinegar and pepper and pulse again until the mixture has become well blended. Pour over salad Makes 1 1/4 cups.

Walnut-Yogurt Dressing

1/2 cup yogurt
3 tablespoons white wine vinegar
1 1/2 teaspoons Dijon mustard
1 clove garlic, chopped
1/2 teaspoon dried chervil
2 teaspoons walnuts, chopped
1/4 teaspoon salt
3 tablespoons walnut oil

Put the yogurt, vinegar, Dijon mustard, garlic, chervil, walnuts, and salt into a food processor. Pulse the food processor until all the ingredients are well blended. Add the walnut oil and pulse for five seconds. Pour over salad. Makes 1 cup.